We want to dedicate this book to:

...s team!
May the
love of our
Lord and the
joy of this sport
be in your hearts
now and forever.

My two sweet sluggers
Chase and Luke.
I am your biggest fan! Play hard
for the glory of God.
Kathryn

"Children are a gift from God; they are His reward."
Psalm 127:3

Lauren, Julia & Katherine,
three amazingly talented
and incredibly beautiful daughters.
Your gifts are many.
Ana

We are grateful beyond words to the following family & friends whose passion for this project have made this incredible journey one of countless blessings. Keeping our eyes on God, and patiently awaiting His perfect timing, you have all been valuable players in _The Spirit in Baseball._ This game could not have been played without you.

♥Blessings,
Kathryn & Ana

This book belongs to:

_____

For: Toryn
    Landen
         &
      Gracyn

May you always play the game
His way! ♡: Blessings.
              Kati Ann

The Spirit in Baseball

Written and Illustrated by
Kathryn Nixon and Ana Boudreau

Cross Training Publishing

Copyright 2008
ISBN: 978-1-929478-73-6
www.crosstrainingpublishing.com
The Spirit in Baseball / Kathryn Nixon and Ana Boudreau
Published by Cross Training Publishing
Kearney, Nebraska 68847
Distributed in the United States and Canada by
Cross Training Publishing

The Holy Bible
New Living Translation
People's Parallel Edition
Tyndale Copyright 1997

The Holy Bible
New Living Translation
Compact Edition
Tyndale Copyright 1996, 2004

A Special Thank You To:

Our beloved husbands, Trot Nixon and Mark Boudreau,
for their constant support, and to our entire families for their
encouragement and prayers.

Kim Olinger, Carlos Perez and our friends at Image Monster
Walt Day
Kenny Dickerson and SEAM Ministeries
Tara Moore
Debbie First
Tina Jacobson
Mike Flaherty and our friends at Walden Media
Wina Woodberry
Ron & Jackie Pegram
Bobbe Evans
Jackie Kendall
Donna Otto
Don and Marcia Christensen
Gordon Thiessen
Jose Perez and Sally Evans

FAITHFULNESS • PEACE
PATIENCE • KINDNESS
GOODNESS • SELF-CONTROL
LOVE • GENTLENESS • JOY

Just as our Heavenly Father hides the "fruit of the Spirit" within our hearts, we have hidden God's created fruit for you to seek throughout this book.

"But the fruit of the Spirit is love, joy, peace, patience, kindness, goodness, faithfulness, gentleness and self-control."

Galatians 5:22-23

The Spirit in Baseball

ve

OVE my teammates. They are my friends. We spend a lot of time in the dugout together!

mans 12:10 "LOVE each other with genuine affection, and take delight in honoring each other."

y

team shouts with JOY when a teammate hits a home run in the ninth inning to win the game.

lm 126:2 "We were filled with laughter and we sang for JOY."

ace

yer gives me PEACE to do my best. I join my teammates in prayer before each game.

hessalonians 3:16 "May the Lord of PEACE Himself always give you His PEACE no matter what happens."

tience

n PATIENT and happy to wait until it is my turn to bat.

mans 8:25 "But if we look forward to something we don't have yet, we must wait PATIENTLY and confidently."

ndness

e KIND words to comfort a teammate who just struck out.

verbs 3:3 "Never let loyalty and KINDNESS leave you! Tie them around your neck as a reminder. Write them deep within your heart."

oodness

o my best to be GOOD to others. I congratulate the other team if they win the game.

hessalonians 5:15 "...Always try to do GOOD to each other and to all people."

ithfulness

n FAITHFUL and believe I should practice my hitting and catching each day. This helps me be the best player God knows I can be.

e 16:10 "Unless you are FAITHFUL in small matters, you won't be FAITHFUL in large ones."

ntleness

my teammates give each other a GENTLE pat on the back for encouragement before we take the field.

esians 4:2 "Always be humble and GENTLE."

elf-control

e SELF-CONTROL by not losing my temper when I strike out or lose the game.

ter 1:13 "Think clearly and exercise SELF-CONTROL."

"Love each other
with genuine affection,
and take delight in honoring
each other."

Romans 12:10

I *Love* my teammates. They are my friends.
We spend a lot of time in the dugout together!

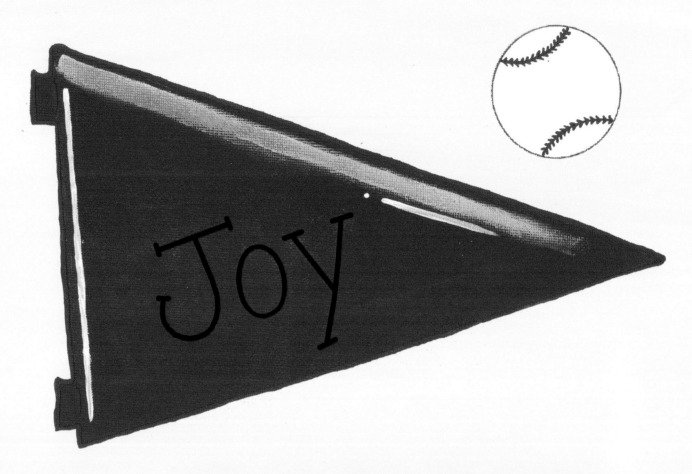

Joy

"We were filled with laughter
and we sang for Joy."

Psalm 126:2

My team shouts with *Joy* when a teammate hits a home run in the ninth inning to win the game.

ANGELS 0 1 2 0 0

SAINTS 0 1 0 2 0

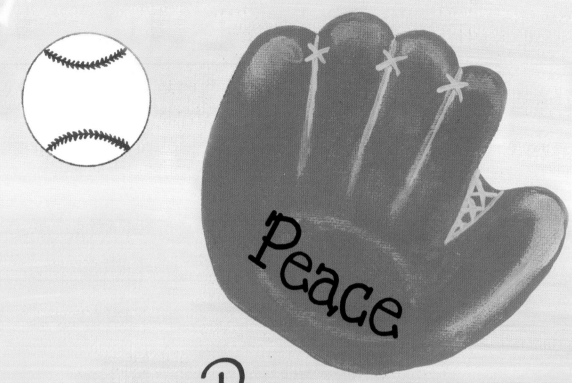

May the Lord of Peace **Himself always give you His** Peace **no matter what happens."**

2 Thessalonians 3:16

Prayer gives me Peace to do my best. I join my teammates in prayer before each game.

PATIENCE

"But if we look forward to something we don't have yet, we must wait *Patiently* and confidently."

Romans 8:25

I am *Patient* and happy to wait until it is my turn to bat.

"**Never let loyalty and** *Kindness* **leave you!**
Tie them around your neck as a reminder.
Write them deep within your heart."

Proverbs 3:3

I use **Kind** words to comfort a teammate who just struck out.

"...Always try to do Good
to each other and to all people."

1 Thessalonians 5:15

Goodness

I do my best to be **Good** to others.
I congratulate the other team if
they win the game.

FAITHFULNESS

"Unless you are Faithful in small matters you won't be Faithful in large ones."

Luke 16:10

"Always be humble and Gentle."

Ephesians 4:2

Gentleness

All my teammates give each other a Gentle pat on the back for encouragement before we take the field.

"**Think clearly and exercise** Self-control."

1 Peter 1:13

Self-control

I use Self-control by not losing my temper when I strike out or lose the game.

Trot Nixon

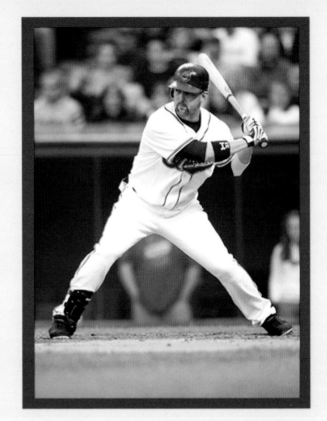

From a very young age these virtues were placed on my heart and greatly influence how I live my life. The fruit of the Spirit has helped me become a better person on and off the field. No matter how much success or failure comes my way I know I can face it with God's help. I will be able to handle situations the right way with the gifts of the Holy Spirit living within me. Each of these virtues will mold you into the person and player that God wants you to be.

About the Authors

Kathryn Nixon. Kathryn, former associate producer for ESPN, graduated from Peace College and North Carolina State University with a BA in Communications and minor in Journalism. Married to Trot Nixon, Professional Baseball player and 2004 Boston Red Sox World Series Champion, and the proud mother of Chase and Luke.

Kathryn, along with her husband, Trot, both have a desire to touch the lives of children with the knowledge and experience of Christ's love. Kathryn has an intense passion to gather children into the kingdom of God by planting His Word in their hearts at an early age.

Ana Boudreau. Ana, artist & muralist, graduated from the University of North Carolina at Chapel Hill with a B.A. in English Literature. Married to Mark Boudreau, and blessed with wonderfully athletic girls. Ana treasures the opportunity to co-author a children's book that has the power to instill God's values in the day to day lives of families, including her own.

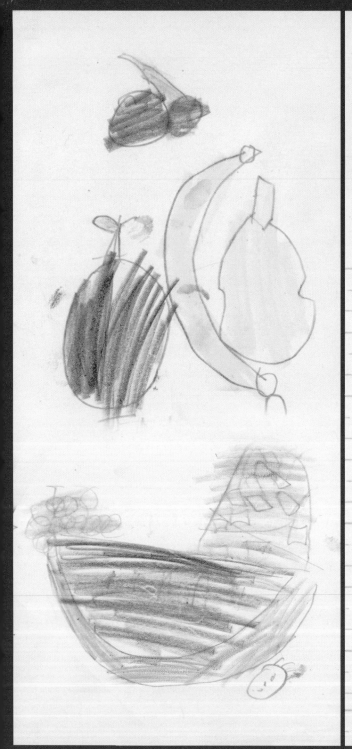

Thbe fruit of Spirti
Love joy peace patience
kindness goodness faithfulnes
gentleness and self-control.
Galatians 5:2223

Chasem

A Baseball Prayer

Dear God,

Help me to be a good sport in this game of life. I don't ask for an easy place in the line-up. Put me anywhere you need me. I only ask that I can give You 100% of all that I have. If the hard drives come my way, I thank you for the compliment. Help me to remember that you never send a player more trouble than he can handle. Help me, O Lord, to accept the bad breaks as part of the game, and may I always play the game on the square, no matter what the others do. Use me as an example of Christ through Your fruit of the Spirit. Help me to study Your Book so I'll know the rules. When I hit a home run or get a triple play, strike a player out or catch the farthest ball, let me always remember, to You be the glory. God, if the natural turn of events goes against me and I'm benched or get struck out, please help me to rely on You and Your Holy Spirit to trust that you are in control of everything. It is my desire to glorify You in all circumstances. And dearest Father, when I finish the final inning, please fill me with gratitude knowing it is a gift just to play the game. All I want is to believe in my heart that I played as well as I could, and that I didn't let You down. In Jesus' name, Amen.

The Chaplain's Digest
Author Unknown

In loving memory of Tip Kincaid

Autographs

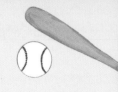